If the Rivers Run Free

Written by
Andrea Debbink

Illustrated by
Nicole Wong

PUBLISHED by SLEEPING BEAR PRESS™

Think about this when you walk down the street:

There could be a river right under your feet.

The world's threaded with rivers—over, under, and through.
They weave through our lands and our history, too.

They begin life as raindrops and snowmelt and springs,
and race through the earth doing marvelous things.

Rivers' currents carve canyons.
They nourish the trees.

Their floods fill the wetlands,
rippling blue in the breeze.

Their waters feed otters and turtles and trout,
and guide flying birds from the north to the south.

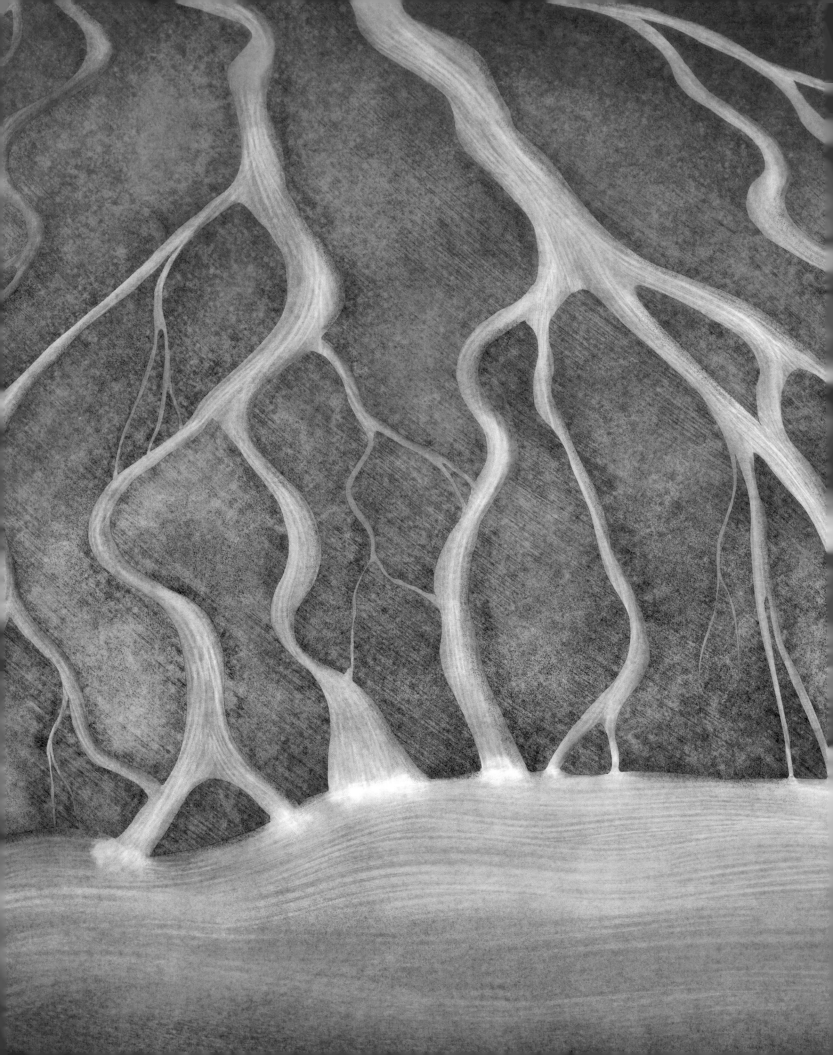

Their voice is a song as they flow to the sea,
when the rivers run wild
and the rivers run free.

But deep in the past when our cities were new,
people needed fresh water—so what did we do?

We built towns on rivers, on rapids, on streams,
and water gave life to our days and our dreams.

Rivers carried our cargo.
    They helped our crops grow.

Then they powered our lightbulbs
        and made the world glow.

Each city grew and then spread like a maze,
sprouting smokestacks and buildings and cramped alleyways.

Our rivers worked harder than ever before.
We took all they gave, yet we still wanted more.

We somehow forgot what rivers could be.
We muffled their music,
blocked their paths to the sea.

We filled them with garbage.... They gave us disease.

They flooded our streets.... We cut down their trees.

Something had to be done.

So the thinkers and tinkers (the best in the land)
stood high on the banks and said:

"We have a plan!

These rivers are trouble, as all of us know.
We're better without them.
These rivers must go."

"But we can't stop the rivers, so here's what we'll do:
We'll trap them in tunnels to hide them from view."

They captured the currents,
and green turned to gray
as the rivers' bright habitats faded away.

From **New York**

to **London**,

from **Moscow**

to **Seoul,**

ancient rivers were buried
and locked up below.

And for a while it worked.

People made progress (or that's what we thought).

Some things
got better—

while some things
did not.

And as the years passed, the old tunnels went *crack*.
It was harder to hold all the strong rivers back.

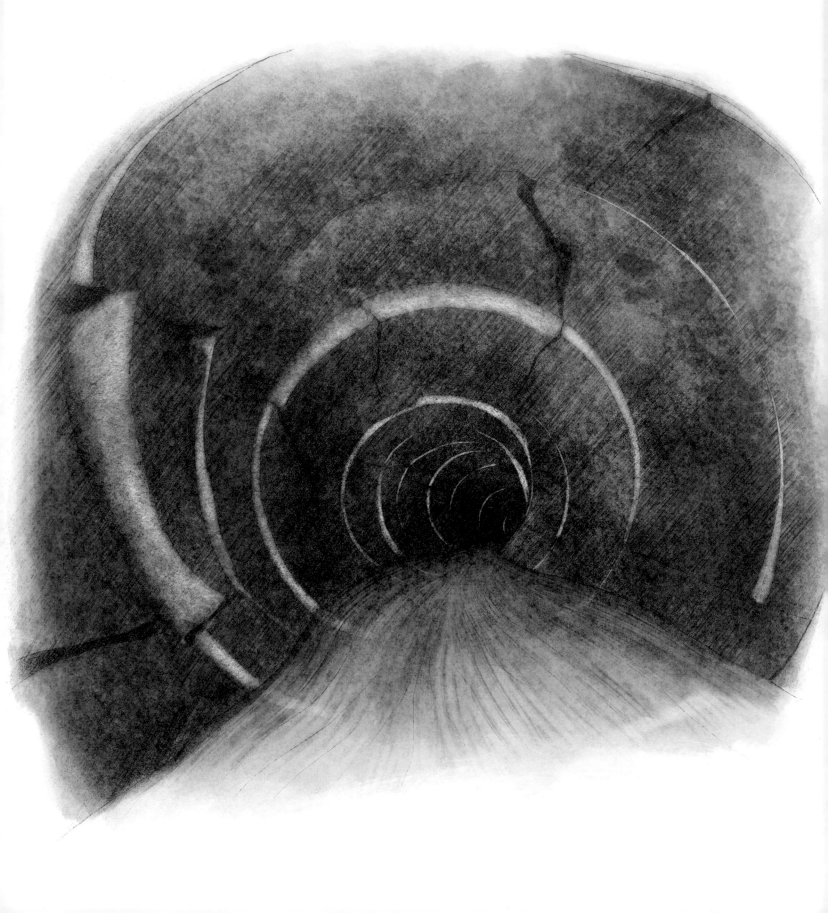

To make matters worse,
when the rain fell in sheets
the rivers still rose and then flooded the streets.

Something had to be done.

So the thinkers and tinkers (and naturalists, too)
peered into the depths and asked:

"What should we do?"

"These rivers are special; they can't be ignored.
What if their habitats could be restored?"

"Imagine a city where bold rivers run,
where they swirl and they sparkle and sing in the sun."

"And think of the good things these rivers can do,
the worlds they'll create, the life they'll renew."

"They can help us through floods and with heat and with drought—
but they can't if they're trapped.

We must let them out!"

It started in **Zurich** with old mountain streams,

then spread like a ripple from **Auckland** to **Queens**.

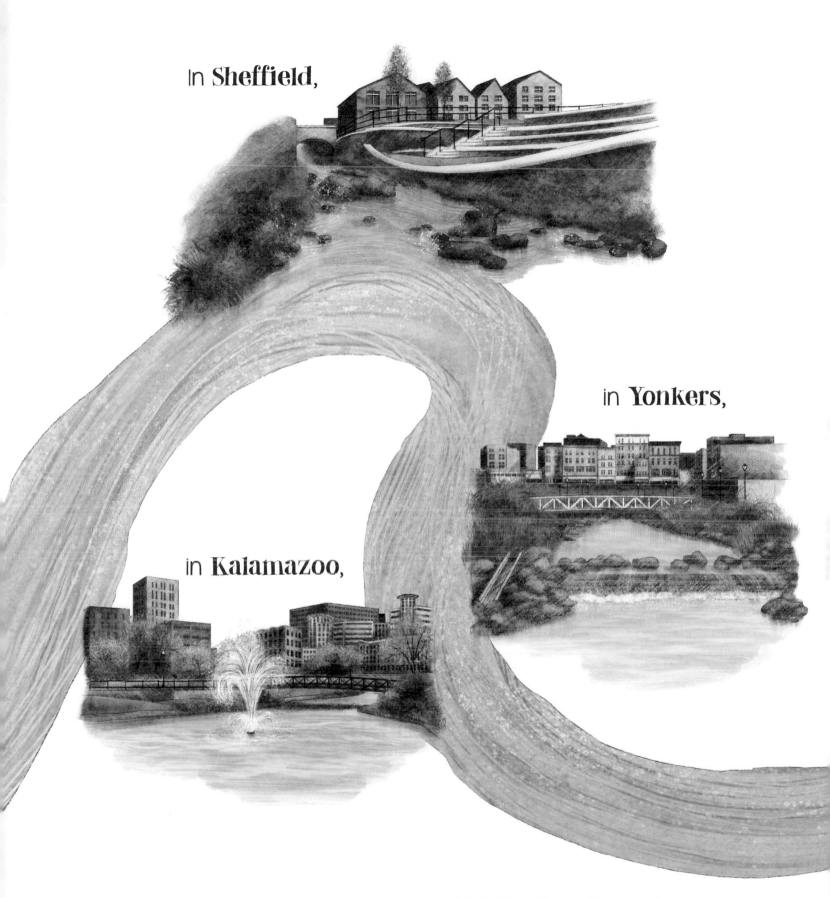

In **Sheffield,**

in **Yonkers,**

in **Kalamazoo,**

people blasted the tunnels and let the light through.

A world that was lost
         soon began to gain ground.
When wonders go missing,
         they can sometimes be found.

And now in those cities where blight used to be
is the rippling new song of a river set free.

There are plenty of places where rivers still hide,
where sewers and streets keep them locked up inside.

We can make different choices and learn from the past.
We can care for our cities *and* nature—at last.

So think about this when you walk down the street:
There could be a river right under your feet.

Then imagine the wonders,
        the world that could be;
you will see it yourself,
        if the rivers run free.

The Wonder of Rivers

Rivers make life possible no matter their size or strength. Some rivers are wide with slow, powerful currents. Others roar over rocks and spill into waterfalls. And the smallest rivers are known by other names like streams, creeks, or brooks. All living things—from humans to the tiniest fish—need water to survive. That's one reason that rivers are so important to life on Earth. But providing drinking water isn't the only thing that rivers do. They have another big job. Rivers, with their flowing fresh water, create habitats (places to live, eat, and grow) for plants and animals. And these habitats aren't just underwater. Rivers also form habitats like swamps and marshes. And the land that's along rivers often has rich soil where forests can grow.

Human Habitats

Rivers create habitats for humans, too. They provide drinking water, transportation, food, power for electricity, and places of beauty and rest. In fact, the great and small cities of the world would not exist without rivers. In England, people long ago built towns on the River Thames and the small rivers that flow into it. Eventually these towns grew and grew until they joined together to become one big city, London. In the United States, New York City grew from a small Dutch trading post to the largest city in the country because of the Hudson, East, and Harlem Rivers. And many other cities throughout the world—Moscow, Seoul, Cairo, Shanghai, Nairobi, Paris— first began as small communities along riverbanks.

Hidden Rivers

But over the centuries, as cities grew, it became harder to keep rivers healthy and clean. People and industries polluted rivers. In many places, urban (city) rivers became open sewers, full of garbage, human waste, and germs. The water-filtering plants, shade trees, natural riverbanks, and flood-reducing wetlands were destroyed— and the effects were often disastrous. The germs in the rivers caused outbreaks of disease. The polluted water was undrinkable and the garbage-clogged rivers would flood during storms. Beginning in the late nineteenth century, people thought one of the solutions to these problems was to bury rivers. Cities around the world paved over their urban rivers, forcing the water to flow through sewers, tunnels, and culverts.

Setting Rivers Free

Burying rivers was really only a temporary solution. As cities grew and paved over more land, the buried rivers flooded once more because there was less soil and plants to soak up rainwater. In the 1980s, people in Zurich, Switzerland, and Berkeley, California, had a new idea for how to take care of urban rivers and streams: dig them up and restore their natural courses aboveground. In Zurich, city leaders hoped that aboveground streams would slowly drain and filter rainwater through soil, instead of quickly sending it to costly wastewater treatment facilities. In California, landscape architect Douglas Wolfe proposed unearthing part of an urban stream to beautify a new park and create habitats for plants and wildlife. Wolfe used the word "daylighting" to describe the project, because they unearthed a buried river and brought it back into daylight. Over the next few decades, more and more cities around the world used the process of daylighting to restore rivers and streams.

The Future of Urban Rivers

Today, people have realized there's another benefit to daylighting urban rivers and streams: it helps communities deal with the effects of climate change. As a changing climate causes more frequent heavy rains, urban rivers can filter rainwater and create wetlands to help provide flood control. Freshwater habitats like wetlands can also store water during drought and slowly refill aquifers, underground water-storage areas. As global temperatures rise, urban rivers can also lower the air temperature of surrounding areas. And rivers provide habitats for threatened wildlife, not to mention recreation and beauty for people who live in cities. Daylighting urban rivers is an idea that addresses the mistakes of the past and meets the challenges of the present and future.

For Reiko–thank you for bringing my
words and ideas into the light

–Andrea

To Q. R.

–Nicole

Sleeping Bear Press™

2395 South Huron Parkway, Suite 200
Ann Arbor, MI 48104
www.sleepingbearpress.com

Printed and bound in the United States.

10 9 8 7 6 5 4 3 2 1

Library of Congress Cataloging-in-Publication Data on file.

ISBN 978-1-53411-278-0